The Moon's Children

The Moon's Children

Poems by

Michael Jennings

Cover design by Shay Culligan

ISBN: 978-1-952326-08-0

Kelsay Books
502 South 1040 East, A-119
American Fork, Utah, 84003

For Suzanne and Shane

Acknowledgments

Poems included here originally appeared in The *Beloit Poetry Journal, Birmingham Review,*
Bottomfish, The Chattahoochee Review, The Comstock Review, The* *G. W. Review, The* *Southern Review* and *Tar River Poetry,* and many were also included in *Crossings: A Record of Travel, New and Selected Poems,* winner of the Central New York Award for Best Poetry Book of the Year in 2016.

Contents

A Circle of Seasons

Before Speech

A Circle of Seasons

Where in this snow can I pick a rose for her
—Ghassan Zaqtan, "Other Conversation," trans. Fady Joudah

For You I Invent the Sun

1.

This, of course, is what money won't buy, this
hip-to-hip, two-centered circle, drift
and drift—you in front, provocative
as a pomegranate, me in front, hearing
echoes—your footsteps filling mine
the way perhaps snow fills the tracks
of caribou, keeping the wolves off. We're
birds of a feather. Our minds veer
and arc on the same air. It's open season here
on sun and wind, and I'm wearing my license
conspicuous and on my sleeve.

2.

We scuff and boot the leaves like six-year-olds,
grin like raccoons. *These are years,* we say,
*shed like snake skins—doomed, irrelevant,
beautiful.* Miles or years, we've walked
forever here, you and I, putting on
or shedding each other like light or leaves,
the traffic hushed and distant. We feel exotic
as the names of these lakeshore towns we walk in,
the water quiet, leaves falling, the light quixotic.
It's all new. You're new—taut and muscular
as a spring colt claiming his first field.
I'm new—grinning ear to ear, hearing windmills.
Death is new here, too, and moves like water underfoot.

3.

We drift in October light through the rose garden,
all the roses gone. Clothed in purple and black,
you're naked. Naked, raspberries and cream,
you're clothed. It's magic. For you I invent the sun,
feel tragic, drive it to your doorstep
in a long yellow cab, stand there, hat in hand,
like some foolish figure in a thirties' flick—

your hair darker than any back-row seat.

4.

You talk, stoop, pick weeds, say *the sky
has breadth.* I say *birds have scissored
it to death,* but I'm dazzled anyway.
It's late fall. The birds look hungrier.
You say you're leaving your husband anyhow—
for all his good, for all my bad.
Standing against a tree, your hood up,
your half-moon smile floating somewhere
below the hairline, I imagine you grew there
whole, yesterday perhaps, dew-like, and I
kiss you, feel shy, boyish—hungry
the way the old birds must
who know they won't get south.

5.

It's mid-winter and the crunching underfoot
sounds rare, precious. You're
purple and yellow. I'm fatigue L.L. Bean
gray-green. The six years between us though
is hardly May and January,
and I'm dazzled by purple and yellow
and can outrun you anyway.
You admit now, though, cold hurts,
for all your tough talk. I should admit
what…for all my tough talk?—that my wife
writes, calls, cries, argues, accuses? Indeed
this crunching underfoot *is* precious—glass
or ice. It's January. It will soon
be May. Our rooms are white and beautiful
and bloom with plants.

6.

Your mother calls, sends chocolates, prays—
makes me feel like the anti-Christ. And
it's true enough I come from a land
of sand and stone, and never put much trust
in trees or green. (In my mind's eye
I always return
to the same rock ridge, almost abstract now
in the blind revision of its lie—
a dark saw-blade raised against blue sky.)
But here, your walk is so much like the sun
or prayer, I must stoop
and touch the place you've stepped, knowing
come spring, something will grow there.

7.

Today bright sun makes blue sky and white birds
pure blue, pure white, barely visible
as we squint and almost stumble
in the pure light.
                         Yet we feel entitled here
as tourists, say, who've paid their fare,
though never dreaming it would look like this.
Beguiled by the low cant of foreign tongues,
we're half afraid some blunt truth in our own talk
will startle us back to earth, bring the dream
crashing like glass about our ears.
                                             But this
is mid-March,
                         when the wind blows and the domed sky
holds,
            when small nests of clustered stones
nosing into wind on the iced canal
rise and become birds.
                                   This is the season
of the long white distance,
                                         when seeing
is much like blindness, blindness like pure sight.

8.

You say, *You are the magician, I but the source.*
Who could top that? Who, mid-stride,
could help but feel the joy
of fear stutter his heart
like cloud-shadow. We have walked
a long time. It is growing dark. I wish

to take you in my arms. I wish to say
to the child we will one day make,
You grew here, among sun and wind
in the gathering dark. I wish to say,
Your mother was taken
for goddess
among stones, among these circling
and calling birds,
                  and they were not far wrong.

9.

We have, I think, no word for this thin-aired
quiet full of light, through which we drift
like new ghosts
risen to Elysian Fields—the still, green lakes
somnolent as deep thought. It's the day
before Easter. The fishermen
standing on the firm bank
wave their fly-rods like bright wands
toward dark depths
where once new life must have climbed, sloth-like
into a dream of sunlight,
and where now loud children and willing dogs
are all smiles, wagging tongues,
sinew and muscle.
Today we talk less, think more.
Today we smile at all that is sensuous
and literal.

Trees

Today they've come back from the snow—
their dream-walk that began in December—
and are settling in along the ravine
where the creek runs, shaking the fatigue
from their bones, talking softly among themselves.
In a week the elders will speak in tongues.
In two they'll be chanting.
Muskrat will hum.
In a month the blue flower of the lake
will break from her icy spell.

Fog

We woke
to cathedrals
of fog—spires, robes, angels—
valhallas of choral voiced silence.
Its breath obliterated farms,
rode the lake's abyss like a warship.
It took the antlers of trees as its standards.
It marched north along roads
whose cars blundered over ridges
like sleepy cattle. Crocuses
brightened like tiny suns
in the sulfurous galaxies of mosses.
On the second day, it lost pomp and contour.
Drum-silent, it lay moiling over hills in listless aftermath.
It clung to our eye-corners like sooty laundry.
By the third day, the tittering of birds was strange.
Their calls vibrated through invisible holes in our bodies.
Our mouths hung stupidly open—our eyes
merely the shifting mirrors of fog. Our hearing
crept out over fields without hope or longing.

The Mountain

The mountain
at the south gateway
of our glacier lake (still white as satin
in late March) is more glorified hill
than mountain,
                but with the sullen blue presence
of mountain, a sort of brow ridge
thrust up from the softer brown thighs
of the other hills—
                bouldered in Pleistocene sleep,
a hill, like Cezanne's, a man
could walk around for years
and get lost in, his eye cutting
narrow goat paths of perfect
clarity.
      So hill becomes mountain
in a vibration of eye waves, in the forgetting
of tedious plains thrust up out of
sea bottom shiftlessness—
                leans hard
in the wind, poised toward some moment
it has lost all track of.

Geese

Over hills russetted by late sun
and the silent underfires of hard winter
the geese rise

they rise over yesterday's white lake,
today a sudden fiery blue,
into coppery, blood-thirsty, perfect sky.

Suddenly I understand their struggle with sun—
it is a wound, their wound. They are bathed in blood
as they rise, necks craned, shuffling, regrouping,

finding their bearings, gathering the sun's power
into their left eye and along their immaculate, outstretched
identical bodies, while below them

the jesterings of black birds in twos and threes
ape their gigantic herding, tittering
at the titanic effortings, swooping and plunging

but wishing them well—or not well
but farewell. While I, chilled and breathless,
take my own chance in the last light

and dance with the oldest tree
on my property, a twisted old apple, all elbows
and shudderings, beaks and talons, a crone

of unparalleled eloquence and elongations,
simperings and croonings, a cackling
of refracted lights and reddening shawls,

burnt siennas, rising as the geese rise
and dancing to the goose's song
until the geese are gone.

He Just Walked Out

sloughed into the dark in his big black body
and did not come back. His fine-furred ears
fluttered as usual at the night's touch.
He slunk slowly down each wet step,
tail testing the air-chills, coiled
at the first touch of grass, then shape-shifted
into the black.
                        He was something to look at,
Bagheera in miniature, with the subtlest
coppery rivers cascading through the black
forest of fur, eyes saffron-speckled
in a dark tiger's face
from a fairy tale.
                        He slept lordly in the sun
on the couch back, or dangled his tail-tip
over the edge for the puppies to swat,
needling them back with a single extended claw
glinting daggerish from a black velvet glove.
Or rolled on his back and taught all five or six
from each litter, for years, the delicate art
of disembowelment.
                        He had humor it seemed,
or even something like love's patience
when he snaked his way among the lewd lumps
of our sleep, to nag us back gently
from the forest of dreams to the sharp-scented
fact of his cat bowl.
                        But he was never ours
any more than the wind or the bird cries.
He'd come back bloodied and satisfied
after days on his own, sleep a day
and a half, and then wake with kittenish
cuddliness.

We'd taken his testicles,
the jewels of his most absolute being,
so it was not entirely the treacherous
lure of sex that drove him, but perhaps
sex sublimated into the godhead night,
lure of star and shadow, death-cries,
life-pulse, drew him to the black edge
of himself,
                   and now I feel him gone,
eyes lusterless and receding among
the hundred similar dead eyes of spring.
He walked out on Good Friday.
Easter brought us the first real spring.
A pair of sparrows is nesting in the small
juniper so close to the house
they too must know he's gone.
I walk out to feel the night air's
soft indifference, to relish its furred face.
What I call my property is being divvied up
differently tonight, fur and feather and bone
in the twisted paths of moonlight.
The bright eyes laugh, winking across the lake.
The stars dive one by one to drown
and be reborn.
                   And everywhere whispers
in the telepathy of time and distance:
the cat, the cat.

March Invitation

Today every tree
a hand of withheld fire,
twisted and passionate against the sky—

Rain back to snow, indecisive,
gusts into a sleety, crow-battering wind
combing lusterless scraggy hills,

sifting the sick fields—loam-scent
rising like a witch-brew elixir
from the crushed pterodactyl skull
of last year's robin.

O ravenous mouth making trees shiver,
the black hearts shudder—

If they knew the glad-hand light of summer
working them like a politician full of promises,
how could they forget in their slag-sleep
this whispery touch, this tingling wakefulness
under the dark dreaming magma of sky?

But their amnesia grows perfect again—
O schoolgirls in the hands of the March wind!

I See You Bend Down

in the garden of pain, the garden of spring,
your after-frost loam-blackened fingers
rooted in roots, dreaming the furred shoots
and delicate unfoldings
of dewy lipped angels attuned to the stars,

and some jungle in me starts growing,
some man of leaves gone slitty-eyed
with cunning, who scans the sky
for a new pale moon

to catch tonight
in the arms of the hairy
old forest—
                    dark mangrove, tall cypress.

Hawk

Dark-rumored inkling of air-chills,
pulsing pupils, the whole hill
monastery-still, a tilting
cliff's edge empty
reckoning—blue water, blue sky.

Ponderous, as if in chains,
attended by black birds, he rises
out of the tree-fringe
hoisted by huge shoulders, granite facemask
blank as an angel's

over the flapping canopy of lake
unwavering and undeterred, past lake rim and horizon
into miraculous high noon
where he who owns nothing, not shadow or hunger,
absolves utterly,

becomes nothing—all shadow, all hunger—
the eye-scorching sun unmasked in its bottomless plummet.

Solstice

This afternoon green, angel-winged, shimmering
summer is upon us, a solemn shadowed, silky
sibilant rejoicing of gnats and dragonflies
in heart-throb stillness.

Only the purr of her engines, in full throttle,
disrupts the fish-silence of stars, the Scheherazade
dawn-silvering, moon-mingling, dusk-moiling
blossom of the lake, my son's face

rapt in the reflected bauble of the world.
We fall down like the stars and we die
mutters the machinery of the green woods,
inventing the full weight of the sun,

its canopied light, wing-pulse murmurings.
We rain down like the sun
                              and he smiles, he smiles.

Raccoon

Days past death, he was decomposing
in a ditch by the roadside,
body gossamered by maggots,
haloed by shed, fine fur,
the black swoon of his limbs
grease for the black oil of earth,
his head no longer head
but the mask of an angel's
upward gaze, the shrunk hands
supplicant.
        Out of the murderous
innocence of midnight, he'd come
strolling, with hands of a jewel thief,
eyes of a gypsy—knocked dead
in a moment.
        The dawn did not mourn him
but lit up the last silvering of his pelt.
The crows pecked at him and savored his eyes.
The maggots swarmed him.
All that pilfering would end soon.
By morning, the curved struts of his keel bone
would house only wind crossing
the leeching black ooze of his emptiness.

Passage

Into the shadows and a little beyond,
your dream—leaping black dancers
burying the sun,
                low river absence.
O lost sad body
of ruined chances, gone-vague
rumor of home.
               Into the stone
silence of bones, under the archway of light,
come agony of alder, oath of oak,
solemn presage of elders—
                   to the bagpipe drone
of the smoke-boned mosquito, dancing the tangible sun.

Nightwood

The dogs tell me they've come,
a skin crawling, fur bristling,
alert, faces in the moonlight
statuary stillness, pressuring
a slight yelp from the youngest.

Something come down in the midnight
from behind the hill's eyelid
travels with the patience of the blind,
browses and peers in at us
with unearthly eyes, as though

the lights of our house were hellfire
guarded by wolves, a terror
that lures them out of slow chewing
sidelong glances, flickering
uncertainty, sudden hoof-thump

oaken vigilance—something more near
than heartbeat, but older, antlered,
waist-deep in the sky-deep blackness,
eyes shining perhaps like stars—
ghosts older than the Iroquois

turned back into trees by the dawn.

Always

under the leaves there was death waiting,
despite your tuned, high-voltage body.

Tigers and rivers glide in us nameless
though the day fades and it is never enough.

The poem deconstructing was an old saw
but we made honey in its warm caldron

and I said *love* with the white mouth
of the moonflower, with iridescent suns

of coneflowers flaunting whispery black eyes.
It was summer in the garden where you moved

without burden of self like a cloud, paused,
looked, shifting your glorious haunches

like any happy horse claiming its field—
all heat and hunger and applause.

Nightscape

The lake tonight is river in the sultry south,
still, smoky, under insect chirr
and black, swampy boughs. A single dock light
claims its lance of silver water
that means loneliness, or hope, or beauty's
steely, soft indifference to beauty.
Out there the old river is speaking to no one
and no one is listening. The half moon
rising is pure Islam. Even my bones know
wherever they are is home.

Diffusions of August

Somewhere, I think, there lurks a poem today—
aching perhaps on the horizon
or in the lost last blue sky of summer.

"I stay indoors and spoil another season"
wrote the old master,
searching the moment within a moment

when the present fades
and there is only the present—
to walk forth crippled thereafter.

Bless us with this curse lisp the thick leaves
with their fat shadows, sibyls
of midnight, silvery wombs of the morning.

The spidery breeze on my face
has come its thousand miles.
The tall trees honor me.

I walk among mountains
and know the angels' names.
I drag my lame foot and feel the beggar's shame.

"They want me to wear old clothes…
not walk in the painted sunshine…
but live in the tragic world."

Hail to thee, dark talkers,
shakers of leaves,
whispering still in the soft air,

in the lazy air,
as insects rattled in the golden blaze
when the poem got made.

Scoffers

This morning a wide-fingered hand
crossed the hood of my car
like a great ray—undulant, ghostly,
more mind-shadow across adobe wall
than simple crow wing's sudden dark
against the metal sheen.
                          Later,
shadowy among trees, their calling
unnerved me, creaking like oarlocks,
and their flapping, eavesdropping absences
pestered my eye-corners—laughter
like bitten off blood-oaths
flung loveless to summer skies, undermining
even the jeweled lichens, the great cascading
cliffs of leaves.
                  And now in a boggy valley
atop the mast-high skeletons of elms,
they cluster like thieves on yardarms
or the tattered crest-plumes of buried horsemen
come back over deathless snows
to claim the purple of loosestrife,
psalming greens of the rushes—
the pinwheel turnings of death's rainbow
in each small, malevolent eye.

October Sun

Weeks since the sun came. Now its crescendo
dazzles the landscape in a thunder of wind
and flaming holy trees. By four, it's gone—
from gilded hills, wide-skirted valleys.
And we, changed, like boatmen come back
over the sliding gray river of clouds
having looked into fire—we've danced
tipsy under the red-eyed sun. Nothing
so deadly as winter can happen now,
we have sun's promise.
                          And the leaves?
They too have a promise—to vessel
the whirl of his fire
into the whorl of the earth
with no more than a thin mad whisper to go on.

October Greeting

Who is she who comes on the wind
when the coyotes cry on the black hill
and the stars hang in their million millions?

Her skirts rustle the dry leaves.
The deer trails widen for the moon
to come. Who is she turns the lake

obsidian, the forest nude,
the treetops spikes? Her skin is cold
under her warm breath, in her wedding dress

turned mourning weeds—
mother of hunger, mother of snow—
whom God's dogs greet with quicksilver song.

Ghost Moon

haunted by cries on a November afternoon.
The geese, with their compass needle necks,
their tumultuous hurry

are passing, have been passing
for days. Each with a piece of magnetic field
planted deep behind its sun-fired eye

heading south. Jostled by wind, pelted
by rain. *Unlikely, unlikely*
their cacophonous holler, their harpy wail.

Something of us goes with them,
feels the ebb in the blood tides
and salt marshes, the emptiness, the cold.

The Road Home, November

Twilight needling the eye—the fogged out,
whited out road collapsing
into goblin namelessness, withering
weird trees, half-light lure
of dog and deer
in the treacherous bearded fields—

Giving in to centuries-old, no-world silence—
head down, nape-of -the-neck
bristling attention
to far star-cauldron nothingness—

Papery-skulled, haggard
from the hard-voiced night,
I come to myself
building a fire—webby, ochre light,
oily shadows, elemental
stonehenge geometry of logs, inscrutable
as the star-crossed bones of bison
bruise-blotting the clammy walls of the caves.

Later my son's raw edged ancient crying
and soft-haired nuzzling.

December Sun

With blank regard, December sun
rides low and lemony
behind the stately spars of the hill trees,
a moment's ambivalence
in the stalled, timeless,
shadowless snow.
                    Crows,
somnolent, creaking, resettle
toward the icier dark
of January doldrums. Old earth
withers behind her diamonds
under her diadem of thorns.
                            Despite parade regalia,
medallions and metals, the far trumpeter
will fail and fail
to waken the crocuses.

Dead of Winter

Old one, I have seen your vacant eye.
It was all night sky, a lens of stars.
From the myrtle of my imagination
I made myrrh and the forest scent
of the new moon, the slow columns of light—
winter there in the trees, in the soft
heavy deaths of the snows.

New snow is the light-pealed crystal
of longing winking dead stars, the inlaid,
still swirling trunks of trees etched in ebony,
precisely feathery as a photographer's negative.
It says I am not here with my daylight eyes,

I have come trackless and scentless
as a mirage to this blanche
of purest silver, this black-river calm.
Old stars move in my veins.
I have seen reflected in your eye, old one,

the interminable dead light in the live deer's shadow
and fires flickering in a far field.

A Moment in February

It is the light at the center of every cell.
                                    —Mary Oliver

See how the silky sun floods the ermine fields—
ton on ton of sheer white light
tumbling kid-gloved soft—each sun-swooned tree
transfixed, snow mittened, bowed as in prayer.
These are the plains of Xanadu
tilting skyward, the high steppes of the Horseman.
Or this is upstate New York shaken
by the vast pastness of the heart, journeys leading nowhere
but here—sun on the snow, the slurred fur
of feel. And everywhere, tremulous, a shout

that's only the sunlight
ringing the molten hearts of trees.

Remains

My son guides me up the long hill
squelching in run-off, along trails
narrow as goat paths through the trees
to show me the strewn bones of a deer
nested in her shed shreds of fur,
almost golden, where some wood spirit
laid her to rest, and the coyotes
and crows stripped her, leaving only
a hoof and furred knuckle intact
among a clutter of collapsed ribs.
He shows me the clean white vertebrae,
the pelvis with its odd eye hole,
the knee still attached with some last rope
of sinew.   This is his find, stumbled on
as he tried his new spring legs in a downhill,
helter-skelter run, and stopped, and stared,
and in his eleven-year-old mind knew
that this was the stuff of running
undone, something the receding snow
left for him personally, a sign
of winter's weight.   We eye it together.
We go down on our knees to gather pieces
of the witchcraft mystery. The gray trees
around us are also bones that click
and chatter in the wet wind
of almost spring. The brown limpid eyes
are gone. The crumbling gnarl
of spine, once nerved and tremulous,
is now only a train wreck the grass
will hide in a month's time. We feel
the doorway of earth opening.
We feel the thinness of our skins

and the prickling of short hairs rising.
We know what's at the bottom of things,
how soon the mayflies will be dancing
their measured reels of the evening.

His Mountain Gateway

—for Will Hier

All day death hovered—
coming through weeks of the gray of November—
becoming the friend
who would not last the year

and did not last the week.
The lake of his dream
became a fuming of crystals
and polished obsidian.

The cold deepened and the ice whistled
and the lake thundered
and the scarred ice vanished
and the whitecaps foamed

till spring became a reflection
of olive placidity, browns
transforming to the delicate
hairy greens

of a thousand shades and nuances
before the leaf-loaded abundance
of summer dreamed
purple evenings etched in shadow,

his photographer's eye
honing beauty out of the hard edges
of weather, season
after season drawn on the lens.

And in the long view south
the mountain named for Song
at the gateway between two mountains
that told us we were home—

the gateway
where I imagine him still—
his farmer's trudge—
bull shoulders, dexterous hands—

casting a warm
but slightly squint eye
on life, on death,
and passing by.

Over Dinner We Begin to Vanish

Let me not to the marriage of true minds
Admit impediments.

—Shakespeare

The faces behind our conversation
begin to sag.
In hard light we look bad.
We know what was.
We laugh.
Soon knowing won't matter
and the moon will rise.
     * * *

The moon will rise
into the twin
obsidian lakes of midnight,
one water, one sky, owls
chuffing their bloodlusts. Two pools
suddenly bottomless
will wake in one another's morning.
     * * *

We'll wake in one another's morning
with Coyote's cunning,
Raven's black laugh,
a whole day to do mischief,
shuffle the sign, bend the law,
eons to rearrange
the faces behind our conversation.

River Time

The hills are green with summer,
the lakes cobalt blue and glittering.
Whatever we longed for in March
is here already or forgotten.
Your hair gleaming obsidian
as always, despite a few white renegades,
your body stretches out like a great cat's
or a landscape I never tire of crossing.
When I kiss the small of your back,
I hear the whisper of desert sands,
the rush of young rivers. No one comes back.
No one steps twice in the same body.
Spring was sun on the daffodils
and the time of the new wide sky,
the heart-breaking golds
of the giant willows.
Marry me, marry me
shouted the cardinal in his tall tree
while the goldfinch giggled
I am nothing but light.

Before Speech

Tired of all who come with words, words but no language
I went to the snow-covered mountain.
The wild does not have words...
I come across the marks of roe-deer's hooves in the snow.
Language but no words.
—Tomas Transtromer, "From March '79"

Before Speech

was the wolf pack, the moon's children,
her insignia borne in the whites of their faces.

There was high ground at the heart of their forest
sacred for long sight, steeped in their smells.

There was bow and gesture, a sniff of the ear
that meant home, that meant heart,
that meant abiding mother with her belly in the dirt.

There was signal flashed across space.
There was the will to sing.
Anyone could start.

Alien

Dropped here from outer space,
her eyes infrared scanners,
she wants to be fed and for the world
to go away. She wants to grow feathers
for her star-cruiser
body to glide the rivers of blackness
she'll come to call home.
In her spaceship egg, she was a whole
galaxy, a liquid listening.
Soon she'll learn about the particle snow,
stealing its white loveliness
as her cold cover. Soon she'll learn about death
under the covenant of stars,

but she will call it life,
chanting her flute-songs of exile.

-

Horned Owl

Leaf. Feather. Bone.

Here is the silent wind-whisperer
come home, a midden
of feathers
in a midden of leaves
in the startled up-gust
of the moment.

Click, click the dice of the mouse's
poor bones.

O bleary buccaneer, age-ridden
and world weary
in the circling forest of blood and thunder.

Remorseless as Blackbeard
and as gaudy.

Squandered by the Hundred Millions

his hell-hunks of rotting flesh
left to slough from his bones
like sacrifices to the god of steel,

one and one and one
he died, she died, they all died,
their stunned unreckoning

rose into stars, numberless as stars.
And the night came
lifting him up with his black rage

and gave him back his magical curving horns,
and lifted his mountainous woolly back-skull
onto the still larger mountains of black woolly shoulders,

and polished his small black eyes
and sharp hooves, his thunderous black bones,
and patched his scraggy, reeking beard.

But by morning the tractors had come
and the grasses vanished, and the dust came,
and that was the end of the first day.

Before Fire

there was the cave dream—
a head larger than the cave mouth itself
with small indifferent eyes,
with ears that didn't need to hear much
but its own mumbling
mastication, the slow throb of its heart.
Breath like carrion,
it was a mountain with a cave for a mouth.
It broke bones like twigs.
It was darkness on darkness with a
black mouth hungering.
                            Later
men made a shrine of its skull
and plunged femur bones
into the sockets of its eyes.

Arctic Wolf Couple

Her gaze cast across eons of Arctic time—

her brow chiseled to wind-whistle,
her muzzle tapering like a dancer's ankle.

Her dream that of the light sleeper,
wind walker, dancing the rock crests
like plumes of snow—

(his, full-bellied, patriarchal,
the drum-beat hunt, the slow spring rain).

His cheek presses her nape,
his ears tuned forward.

Their cubs play nearby. A turkey buzzard
circles, listless.

Winter only a grim recollection.
Long life to come.

Scales

Old bubble brain
floating in primordial ooze—
Turn him on his back
and he sinks into coma,
forgets yesterday, hardly fathoms
tomorrow.

How easily we condescend
in our neocortical glimpse.
He cannot laugh or be sociable.
His one purpose
to go on expanding, to eat
and be filled and eat again.

Mountain ranges grow from his back.
His each scale anticipates
the iron age by eons.
He is the Hindu calendar
written in Braille.
For him it's still the beginning of time.

Expressionless as God.
His undulant tail
the shadowy frond of some first fern
the abstract angels dance on.

Old Testament Anointed

testosterone infused King of Sleep—
20 hours in a day!

A great war machine
in the service of its genitals—

devours any cub not his own
to mount mother

like a Myrmidon sacking Troy.

Once boys became men
facing this face—the long stony head

like a great stone ax
fells what it catches, gorges,

hurtles its cough of thunder nightward.

Beluga

What were once perhaps arms have simplified in time
to water wings, undulant and white in a black sea
pearled and catacombed with ice.
                                             Pelvis has vanished,
or is at most vestigial, tapering to feet turned tail fin
in a slow fan of somnolent propulsion,
dream-lazy, ghostly.
                                Her call, her only weapon,
is sonar deadly, a stun gun, prelude
to instant swallowing and digestion, death
under anesthetic.
                           The world of stars and sun
and the hard crust of earth
betrayed her, though she visits still,
white in the white moonlight—
                                       the dome of her mind
grown huge and forgiving in the cave of the sea.

Shadow Creeper, Old Ghost

steps tirelessly through snow-sparkle
and tree-dark, shoulders
rising and falling like wave-crests

of feathered silver, nose forward
and down, sifting pheromones
that mean moose or rabbit

or the tooth-clawed bear—
shifting gravity's center
as a pendulum,

as a man falling
into shock-shifting fore pasterns,
spring-loaded

forward propulsion,
tail no longer a pride-plume
but rudder

and counterbalance, head
heavy-browed tracking device
tuned in and ticking,

feet silent as snow on snow
for hours,
for eons.

Taking It Slow

Methuselah in his mudpack paradise
cools his scales in ooze
and peers out from beneath his dome
in utter indifference:
a world so changed from his youth,
so withered, so shrunken,
he dreams he carries it on his back,
blinking in the slow sun—
lipless, mute as stones or the far stars.

Amazons

A pride of 30 lionesses—single
pre-phalanx wall of blond muscle,
pure infantry—slides in one hunger
through the one darkness, patient
as desert wind, insect heat—
slides motionless as the deep sea
stone minded in its one dream
rivered with tendons.
                    What awaits this
in the brush, in the shadow burrows
and ruts of the night wind, must dream
mouths larger than prairies, frieze
in the moonlight nameless as stars
falling—impala become Impala, warthog
Warthog, its riveting shrill shriek
a shearing of metal—
                    night erupting
into bonfire—claws, teeth, flesh,
kin and carcass—mandarin faces,
sleeked in blood, scarred senile
in the anarchy of kill.

Later they'll greet the dawn,
lolling, licking each other, satisfied
they've kept the universe open,
the tall dead rising.

So Close to the Edge

of his granite, glacier-sheared promontory,
the claws of his massive forepaws
overhang it—
        shoulders, neck, and doleful wedge head
riding the abyss—
        a siren song, wind's nocturne,
the bitter soul's hungering departure.
        All of him goes into it
and upward
until he is only the vanishing host of a voice—
an open question in a Zen listening—
        calling and calling.

Tiger Dance

She is the languid, languorous
disease of the sun, flower
of his passion, hint
of his corruption among shadows.

He comes to her disguised
as her double, only larger,
more impossibly brutal-beautiful—
his face a Paleolithic sun shower.

She in turn turns tiger lily,
all smiles and pussycat frailty
shivery under his touch—
needier, whorier

than his lewdest imaginings—
his great winking anus
laughing at the winking
gay forest above them.

This is he who has hugged
and scarred the trees
as his vassals, whose gape
at her nape is the very vault of heaven.

This is she
who releases him,
brings on the darkness,
leaves him free again to love nothing.

The Sisterhood

come down to water
to bathe their itching tonnage,
with ponderous brows
and wide nostrils,
take in the day with the same
curious poise, long-eared and quizzical,
as the day they washed out
into world, knock-kneed and tottering,
or when world
slides out of them
under the wolfpack's steel trap snarling—

hooves planted deep in the musk
of the wide earth's
beckoning.

Black Leopard

Where she comes down

in a slow boil
of uncoiling muscles,
dropping the last few feet

onto spongy big feet,
rosette points
like black stars on a black river—

we know this place,
deep in our sleep,
moonlight silvering the ancient leaves,

the scarred, inscrutable
dream-mask, ears
like small delicate flowers.

The baboon barks once and is still.
The sambur shift and stamp
in the rasping, dry grass.

They too know the myths of the death tree
and the death shadow, of distant yellow suns
smoldering in the furred midnight.

The Great Mother, After Long Drought

so tiny eyed, so tired, so wrinkle-rivered
in her skin of dust,
has trudged so long in billowing skirts of dust,
knelt fat-assed and humbled as Old Mammy
in chasms of dust—
her great trumpeting trunk following its long instinct
for water.

Now she has come. Leading her cows
into the kingdom of cows,
down long winding rivers of cows,
single-file, dust-smoldering processions—
tusked, vigilant, thunder-shaking—
meeting and touching each
to each in the great milling of cows.

Such soft-handed knowing in that fondling
probing lip! Such fingertip-tender
tickling laughter
behind the preposterously old faces—
Even *elephant* is not word enough!

The rivers are jubilant!
The mud holes grow deeper!
She has come
like a black cloud
bringing a black cloud
to a land like her very skin!

Earth shaker! Bellower! Maker of rain!

Mother of Angels

is dreaming her web—
swings through the firmament
with electron purpose,
trembling feelers—
                    minute mindless astronaut
at her gadgetry, each leg
a violin string
tendering a single blood-note,
each eye
many-eyed with malice—
                    Little Alice
of ice
dangling her lace curtain,
humming primly to her ribbon,
throbbing in the open air
like a suddenly ripped out
heart
        alive to nerve twitches,
death-shouts—
                    herself the toneless ticking
of her eggs.

The Serval, Demure as Nefertiti

can swat down the startled thunder
of a guinea cock
a full six feet in air,

her face in feathers
as behind a Chinese fan.
Long glamorous legs, ears plucking sound

from tiniest twig whisper,
she paints herself into the scrub
with pointillist self-effacement,

still as death for hours.
Or rolls the bowls of her muscles
in hair-trigger readiness.

No mirror-reflecting waywardness—
No hum of thought in the taut strings of her body—
Sloe-eyed gleaming guardian of the field's sleeplessness.

One Paw Poised

the others planted in snowpack,
here is the lost spirit of the moon's cunning,
joy of the hunt, joy of the kill—

who claimed the gothic conifers
before Goths or Vandals
or the Westward Expansion—

who felt the steel trap's
bodiless jaws, the bullet's
invisible fang; twisted in strychnine

bewilderment—
hung upside down
on iron crosses of barbed wire

and died by the myriad
for our sins.
                Now let us praise him.

Black Wolf at Midnight

(after the print by Robert Bateman)

At first we do not see the eyes—
bewitched, bewitching—only trees,

their latticework of iced branches
glittering where moonlight patches

the dark, where any moment centuries
old stone-cold silence threatens

to crack like ice the thin bark
in the eternal click, click

of minerals in the soft shift of wind.
Some moccasined tracker in skins

crouched under stars, cold heart
in his mouth, might have stared out

and seen, for the first time,
the colossal foot—hairy, snow-rimed—

planted too eerily close. Dread
paw of the wolf feathering upward

to where the gray column of leg dwarfs
the wrist-thick trunks of the light-starved

trees. Then fathomless bulk
of black body and mystic gold

eyes latched onto him there in that
first dark. Ours is the more distant

wonder of Art, that he could do this
so stealthily, shrewdly, our eyes

tuned to these eyes, our gaze
fixed to this stare without remorse

or malice, a criminal angel's—
our shadow brother lost in the ages

light years after.

Wolf Song

I return to the river,
my tail plume light as a feather
in feathery wind.
I am the stones' ancestral voices.
I am the wide earth listening.

My girl is my playmate
in a song of Hafez,
quick feet to feed our children,
eyes the color of spring rivers.
See our big tails dancing.

Red sky. Rock ridge. So I travel
and the gold sun honors me,
singer of high places, queen night,
sifter of pheromones.
I scent the leaves and my good bones marvel—

lordly in the far off
nearness, the arrow and the bow.

About the Author

Born in the French Quarter of New Orleans and growing up in east Texas and the deserts of southwestern Iran before graduating from the University of Pennsylvania as an undergraduate and Syracuse University as a Graduate Fellow, Michael Jennings is the author of 11 previous collections of poetry, most recently *Where She Dances* (2020), *Summoning the Outlaws* (2018), *Crossings: A Record of Travel*, winner of the 2016 Central New York Book Award for Poetry, and *River Time*, winner of the 2014 Wells College Chapbook Contest. He is also the 2017 winner of the Miller Audio Award for Poetry offered by *The Missouri Review* judged by Vijay Seshadri.

www.ingramcontent.com/pod-product-compliance
Lightning Source LLC
Chambersburg PA
CBHW031149090426
42738CB00008B/1271